OLABISI ROMEO

THE STRESS FREE MUM

A practical guide for the foundation years

Content

Acknowledgement

My sincere gratitude is to God Almighty for trusting me with this task and inspiring me all the way through. I am the least qualified of men, and I am glad He still uses foolish things to confound the wise.

To my biggest fan and darling husband 'Yomi, for his faithfulness and love to God and me. Thank you for allowing me to follow my dreams. I am sincerely grateful for your tremendous support and prayers.

To my seeds of greatness, my gifts from God, my dear sons, I love you beyond the moon. Thank you for teaching me how to love and for loving me just the way I am.

To my daddy and mummy, Elders Francis and Marian Alaran, thank you so much for all you do. I honour and appreciate you loads. Indeed the foundation you laid for me has contributed to the woman that I am today.

To my spiritual parents, Pastors Sola and Tumise Ewedemi, thank you for being there for me. Most notably, thank you for the prayers and teachings that have transformed my life over the years.

To my family and friends, too numerous to mention, thank you for your love and support. You are simply the best.

Foreword

Motherhood which undeniably is one of the most gratifying and rewarding jobs in the world is undoubtedly one of the most daunting endeavours one can embark upon especially without proper guidance, help and advice.

The journey of motherhood is one in which some of us are already in as women or would embark upon at one point or the other in our lives; and which I daresay, never really ends. It is from the cradle to the grave. I embarked upon mine over twenty years ago, and as I read this book, I consistently found myself wishing this book when I had my first child. It certainly would have made my experience less stressful and chaotic.

In this book, Olabisi has been able to provide a well-structured, well balanced, easy to read piece of research on the difficult yet most satisfying job in the world- Mothering!

She has been able to present this in a down-to-earth yet enlightening and insightful way, which if practised by the reader, will generate fantastic results; the kind of results I have personally seen the author live out in her own life.

Please, have your pen ready to take notes because each chapter has insights, wisdom and advice that will not only help you do a better job at mothering but also aid in making you a more organised and disciplined person all round.

The chapter on "Speak Life" is simply life-giving, and my favourite chapter in the book as I found myself instantly changing my vocabulary.

The practical scenarios and the realistic action plans in each chapter can also help transform the "most stressed" mother into the "most tranquil" one and help revolutionise their experience of mothering into the most enjoyable and worthwhile experience that it is meant to be.

I would like to encourage you that as you read this book, irrespective of what stage you are in your journey of mothering, it is sure to do one thing to you - not leave you the same!

Olutumise Ewedemi
Kings Court Chapel
Milton Keynes, UK.

My Journey

My Journey

Parenting is a role we begin without any job description, person specification or terms of employment. Nothing prepares us for the journey of parenting. On this journey, we encounter the diversions of unplanned interruptions, the roadblocks of sleepless nights, the traffic lights of tantrums, the road bumps of behavioural issues, the potholes of tiredness, the roundabouts of uncertainties and even the road rage drivers of stress.

Well, instead of feeling squashed in a car on an endless journey, we can fasten our seatbelt, appreciate the scenery, take our eyes off the challenges along the way and enjoy our parenting journey. We can also take it a step further and ask, "Could there be an alternative route on this journey?"

As a pregnant young lady, I already struggled with my uncontrollable weight gain and flabby maternity dresses (that was all I could find in the shops in those days), and I certainly did not want to lose any more control. I still wanted to live my life and not blame the joy of motherhood for any dissatisfaction I felt.

I ran (well not really) to my friends, hoping that their wise counsel will lead to my shouting 'Eureka!' but unfortunately, my friends who were already mothers, had (shopping) bags under their eyes. They were too stressed to care less. I didn't bother asking any question for fear of being disappointed.

Maybe if I didn't see their faces, I could boldly voice my concerns, and so I began making phone calls.

Unfortunately, they all didn't have time for me. Well, to be fair they did, at least they picked up the phone, and we exchanged a few pleasantries, but soon it became a three-way conversation. My friends spoke to me, and before I could reply, they yelled at their toddlers who were still running riot late at night. 'This was no use', I thought to myself as I came off the phone.

The following week, I bumped into an old friend while shopping for my soon-to-be-born bundle of joy. She looked calm, and everything (hair, buttons, make-up, etc.) was in place. She looked like the right candidate to quiz about the motherhood journey, but before I could say 'hi', she had told me how she had to abandon her career to take care of her child. She also stressed how she had missed 'adult' company. I didn't doubt that because my dear friend kept me standing in the shopping aisle for close to an hour.

By this time, I could feel my stress levels rising. The apparent rise was not because of the long conversation about everything and anything, but because of worry. There must be a reason why people say the 'joy of motherhood'.

Later that week, I went to church and to my greatest surprise, the once vibrant church volunteers now blamed their children for their inability to serve in the church and attend church meetings hence the decline in the numbers during this weekly departmental meeting. This certainly wasn't the route I wanted to take. There had to be an alternative to my journey, and I had to find it. I was determined to live life, have a full-time career and enjoy parenting. Although I knew the combination of these was going to be difficult, I was determined to eat my cake and have it.

Introduction

Introduction

Let's Talk

"I don't seem to have any time on my hands!"
"I am so tired, can't seem to get any rest yet there is still so much left undone!"
"I never knew motherhood could be so tasking!"
"I am constantly stressed, and my patience is wearing thin!"

Though the list is endless, does it sound familiar? Ever felt you couldn't cope with the mounting pressures of the job, house chores, keeping the family together and raising children?

Do you perpetually feel stressed? Like a pressure cooker waiting to let off steam.
Do you sometimes feel you haven't got any more to give?

Do you wish the days and nights could be longer? Longer days to get things done and longer nights to rest from all the hard work, or are you always 'Thanking God it's Friday', and with a heavy heart welcome Monday morning, wondering where the weekend went (that is supposing you do not work weekends)?

Do you always feel the tug of pressure from:-
❀ Work - too much work, too little pay.

❄ Friends - need more time to keep in touch.

❄ Husband - never seem to meet his needs.

❄ Home - a call for spring cleaning.

❄ Social life - being a hermit isn't rewarding.

❄ Spiritual life - it is time for a deeper walk with God.

❄ Child - patience and an instruction manual will be appreciated.

Yet you can hear the cries welling up within you from:-
❄ Your hair – *'I wonder when you'll go to the hairdressers?!'*

❄ Your fingers – *'It would be nice to have a manicure!'*

❄ Your feet – *'I don't think I'm asking for too much when I say you should take me off the ground for a few minutes, I know you do at bedtime, but an occasional pampering would not hurt!'*

❄ Your body – *'I have tried to tell you over and over again, take a break. I thought the constant headaches would have given you a clue, but that hasn't worked so I might as well spell it out, I NEED REST.'*

Introduction

Interestingly enough, most of the issues that cause us stress end up getting our attention whether we like it or not. However, the problems that get our best are mostly the ones that cry out the loudest and not necessarily those at the top of our priority list.

This is typically the case when we have young children with ages ranging from 0-5 years. At this stage, the children endure and hardly question whatever life throws at them. Thus, the main focus of this book is the foundation stage or early years of the child.

Why the early years?

The Early Years is the best time to shape the child into the adult you want. Children are more receptive to learn and being taught at this age. The 'early years' is the best time to start the way we intend to go on. If we want our children to be respectful at age fifteen, then we ought to begin emphasising respect at an early age.

The early years is also an excellent time to instil spiritual and social values into our children. This does not mean we cannot teach our children at a later time; however, it is the best time because we face less resistance.

Although this book focuses on parenting within the early years, the guidelines shared apply to all ages.

Why Parenting?

It is possible to do a job we despise by going through the motions and keeping at it because of the bills. It is also likely that we please everyone around us for the sake of peace, love and unity; however, when it comes to our children, we fail to stretch ourselves. We struggle to bend backwards and sometimes neglect the search for workable solutions to resolve our stress-related parenting.

Many of us mums may wish pressing a 'play, pause, stop, rewind and fast-forward button' would make motherhood less burdensome. Unfortunately, this is just what it is, a wish. There is bound to be the feeling of stress given the unpredictable nature of parenting.

Though fathers play a significant role in parenting, mothers feel the extra heat because the children spend the most time with them; this is taking into account the ante-natal, post-natal and foundation stages. This excludes cases of single fathers, divorced fathers and widowers solely caring for their children.

Bearing in mind that there are no hard and fast rules on the parenting journey, there are practical steps we can take to ease the burden of motherhood. These would take the pressure off our shoulders and also equip us with the necessary skills to raise exceptional children while enjoying our life.

Introduction

Embedded in these practical steps are biblical principles that have helped to guide me from the stressful to the tranquil path of being a Stress Free Mum.

So who is the Stress Free Mum?

The Stress Free Mum is a woman of faith in a world where fear prevails. She knows there will be challenges along the way but strongly believes there will always be a way out.

The Stress Free Mum faces loads of battles, some big and some small. To the world, battles should end in a win-lose situation, but to her, battles are a win-win situation regardless of the outcome.

The Stress Free Mum is not a woman with zero stress but one who is in control of it due to the greater One on her inside. She is positive and purposeful, with a plan and on a mission. She knows what she can deal with and what causes her stress and so she plans ahead of time and tries her best to be organised.

The Stress Free Mum understands that life comes with stress, yet she doesn't wait to be overwhelmed by it. She prepares beforehand, like a lion waiting for its prey. She refuses to be the prey, and so she prays.

The Stress Free Mum is brave. She is a woman willing to jump, knowing fully well that she has no wings, yet she expects to fly.

Introduction

The Stress Free Mum is an investor. She invests time into herself and her family. She understands that after God, family comes first. She is aware that no career or pay supersedes the benefits of motherhood.

The Stress Free Mum knows she isn't superwoman but a woman with a Super God. She is not perfect. Sometimes she cries, loses her cool, yells, feels overwhelmed, but she holds on to the One who made her a mum. She holds on to the One who has the power to calm every storm.

The Stress Free Mum is grateful for her role. She knows that motherhood is a privilege and not a right. She is on a journey to live her life while enjoying motherhood.

She is a woman with no name or race - she is simply The Stress Free Mum.

Chapter One

Write the vision; make it plain upon tables, so he may run who reads it.

Habakkuk 2:2

(ESV)

Have a Plan

The journey of motherhood should be travelled with focus and determination. It ought to be a purposeful trip leading to a desired destination or goal which for most mothers is to be the best while enjoying the journey.

Planning is necessary before the start of any journey. No one gets on a bus, plane or even drives to an unknown destination. Regardless of how long or short a trip is, a plan is required.

Planning is a necessary tool for goals to be achieved. It is the prerequisite for the achievement of objectives. Planning is crucial if we desire success in any endeavour. It is easy to write down goals yet quite challenging to achieve the set goals without a plan. We are sure to succeed and feel more fulfilled when we plan and work towards our goals.

According to Webster's Online Dictionary, a plan is defined as 'a series of steps to be carried out or goals to be accomplished'. It also refers to having a strategy that propels one to the desired result. Planning is the most effective way of reaching targets and completing tasks. It begins by visualising a goal, which with regards to this book, pertains to de-stressing, raising godly children, living life, loving you and enjoying

---

motherhood.

The importance of planning is highlighted in Luke Chapter 14 verse 28.

For which of you, intending to build a tower, does not sit down and first count the cost, whether he has enough to finish it. Luke 14:28 (NKJV).

If this verse was written exclusively for mothers, I want to assume it will read something like this:-

Dear woman, before you become a mother, take time to think! Think about the kind of mother you would like to be with your children. Take time to identify the skills you will require. Take time to prepare. Prepare in prayer, prepare by reading and prepare by observing godly mothers around you. Arm yourself with all you need, for the journey will be long and never-ending.

Indeed the journey of motherhood is a long one with some bumps along the way. It is easy for us mothers to get caught up in irrelevant activities and merely distractions; however, planning highlights the important and the necessary. It prompts us to ask ourselves regularly,

Chapter One

'Is this taking me closer or farther away from my goal?'
I am sure we have heard the following sayings:-

'If you fail to plan, you plan to fail'.
'If you plan for nothing, you'll achieve nothing'.
'If you aim at nothing, you won't miss your target'.

Imagine waking up on a Saturday morning, you have a shower and brush your teeth (as expected), have breakfast (for those who do), and slump right in front of the TV to catch up on the events of the day. You get up to have lunch and dinner. Then at bedtime, you try to reflect on the goals you achieved for the day. Except all you planned to do was to get up, eat and relax; you would have achieved nothing.

Unfortunately, this trend affects all facets of life, and it can progress on for weeks, months and years. It becomes a complicated case of living life without purpose. Sad to say but the same applies to motherhood. We all hope and pray to be the best stress free mother any child could ever wish for; however, no amount of dreaming will get us there without taking necessary actions.

As godly mothers, our starting point before we plan should be from the place of prayer. Scripture says in Proverbs Chapter 3 verses 5 and 6:-

Chapter One

Trust in the Lord with all your heart. Never rely on what you think you know. Remember the Lord in everything you do, and He will show you the right way. - Proverbs 3:5-6 (GNT)

Trusting the Lord with all our heart is a reminder that nothing else should have our trust but our Lord God. We should believe that God who has blessed us with children is big enough and God enough to help us on our parenting journey as long as we invite Him in.

The above verse says we should 'Remember'. That means we can forget God and leave Him out of the picture once we get preoccupied with motherhood. Hence the need to pray early, even before the babies arrive.

I remember the actions of Manoah, the father of Samson. Once his wife informed him that they were to have a child, he took time out to pray to God. His request was specific. He wanted God to teach them how to bring up the child.

Then Manoah prayed to the Lord, and said, "O my Lord, please let the Man of God whom You sent come to us again and teach us what we shall do for the child who will be born." - Judges 13:8 (NKJV)

The scripture says that God granted his request. If God could do it for Manoah, He will do the same and much more for us too. Like Manoah, our hearts and ears should be hopeful and receptive to what God has to say concerning our children. Once we have received a clear word, then our planning and acting can begin.

The Lord answered me, "Write down what I show you. Write it clearly on a sign so that the message will be easy to read.
- Habakkuk 2:2 (ERV)

So the question is:-

- Have you asked God what His plans are for your child?

- Are you close enough to Him to hear when He speaks?

- What is God saying or what has He said about your child?

- How has God told you to bring up your child?

- What are the parenting skills you require to nurture your child in the way of the Lord?

- What is God saying about you too?

- What kind of parent has God called you to be?

There may be many other questions that the Lord will drop in your hearts as you read this book hence the need to have a pen or pencil to hand, to write down the vision and make it plain. On the other hand, plans and actions are necessary to deal with day to day issues that overwhelm us on our parenting journey. Yes, prayer is good, and it is needful, but prayer without the necessary action is folly. For instance, we cannot pray tiredness away without taking time out to rest.

As a young mum, I did pray for grace and strength, especially when it was a struggle to care for two babies, but I also scheduled the time to rest. I realised that I could only give out what I had.

Once I got cranky and short-tempered, then I knew it was time for a much-needed rest. I have learnt that a stress-filled mum will exude stress-related emotions such as sadness, depression, anxiety, irritability, moodiness and anger. She would most likely take it out on those closest to her; the children. However, once she can dispel the stress-related emotions, there would be room to develop healthier relations with her children. Knowing how to plan against stress will surely get us through challenging circumstances. Failure to plan and act would leave such mothers living a life of regret once the children are all grown up.

But why should we become victims of guilt when we can act now?

From experience, planning helped me eliminate futile activities that clog up time and sap energy, leaving me with a better disposition to deal with issues that would naturally have caused stress. When my older sons were both under two, I realised that motherhood at that point could make me grumpy and drained, but I wanted to be my happy, sane self. I wanted my children to have the best of me and not the rest of me (after a tough day). After much thought, I recognised that making plans and setting goals was the way to go.

I planned for everything. I planned for my daily quiet time. I also had a plan for completing each household chore. There were also plans for shopping for groceries, nap time, mealtime and bedtime.

Life may have seemed too structured at the time, but it was the best way I could cope with no extra hands but my husband's. I remember how I listed out situations or conditions that could cause me stress and then looked for possible solutions to calm or neutralise them. For example, I got stressed anytime my newborn was asleep and there was noise in the background. Everything came to a grinding halt to suit this tranquil being. But what was I to do to handle the situation other than to get him used to noise? And that was what I did. I planned to carry on as usual and to stop walking around the house on tippy-toes. This baby wasn't going to control me anymore. I had to take charge, after all, 'Who's the Mummy?'

Chapter One

Things had to change in my home and so while he slept, his older brother, who was under two, carried on playing. I vacuumed whenever I wanted to, used the food blender and even left the telephone plugged in. Oh yes, that was how much my life had come to a halt when my baby dearest fell asleep.

Of course, it took some getting used to from all of us; however, we got there in the end. And when we did get there, I was no longer stressed out by noise during my baby's afternoon nap time because the origin of that stress no longer existed. The solution worked quite well for me, and I used the time he was asleep to rest or go about my house chores without feeling constrained. This change was one of the best decisions I made with my babies.

My daily plans also included time to pray, time to study the Bible and time for my continuous personal development. I made Habakkuk Chapter 2 verse 2 my watchword. I planned to live my life without limits, even though I was a mum of two babies.

I am grateful to God that I was able to achieve some set goals. These include:-

A sustained prayer life.

The completion of an 8-week evening course.

Chapter One

 The set up of a business and

 Consistently serving as a volunteer in the local church.

With hindsight, there are certainly no regrets. I know for a fact that if I had no plans, I might have crumbled under the pressure of taking on too much, blaming myself for doing too little or wasting time by paying little attention to the important. If I could, you can too and even do much more by God's grace and help.

Our planning should not be restricted to long-term goals but can also feature daily or short-term goals. Short term goals should reflect our significant goals and create the roadmap for our journey. It is the short-term goals that we achieve on a day to day basis that determines how and if we would accomplish our long-term goals.

There should be daily goals, no matter how minute we think they are. Remember it is all about managing ourselves better during early motherhood to exude peace and positively influence our children.

Our plans for the day could be as simple as dedicating some quality time to our children or even time for ourselves. As a mother, what would you like to achieve this year, this month or this week? Our desire to be the epitome of a great mother can begin today. We can achieve the following results if we follow through our daily plans over a certain period:-

❀ Better organisational skills

❀ A more organised and orderly home

❀ More productive time with the children

❀ Better relationship with our children

❀ More time for ourselves

❀ More time for God

❀ A stress-free home and definitely

❀ A stress-free 'you.'

It is pertinent to note that keeping to plans benefits both our children and us. My prayer is that once our children are all grown up, they would say, "I have the best mum, and she made my childhood memorable".

What Some Mums Did

 Juliet is a single mum of two children, a three-year-old and a one-year-old. Being a single mum wasn't by choice, but as we all know, life happens. She embraced her status as a single mum and promised to make the most of her life with her children.

Juliet, who had no extra help, worked full time from Monday to Friday while her children attended a Day nursery school about ten minutes' walk from their home. Like every other mother, she struggled with parenting, mainly because of her energetic pair; however, she was determined to bring her children up in the way of the Lord. This desire led to her planned daily prayers with her children.

Juliet also struggled to go shopping with her children because of their usual temper tantrum during this weekly activity. She was always left embarrassed when she watched her children roll around the shop floor as if they were competing for who could shout the loudest, just because she refused to put another unnecessary item in the shopping trolley.

In her bid to cope with stress, Juliet planned to change her shopping experience. She shopped online and opted for home deliveries. By doing this, she was able to use her time and energy effectively.

Given her busy weekdays, Juliet planned to make quick and easy meals during the week to allow her to spend more time with her children after work.

❋ Abi is a stay at home with a young baby. Although married, Abi made her plans around the unpredictable nature of her baby. She planned to rest or sleep whenever her baby was fast asleep during the day, so she was not too tired to cope with the night feeds. Her hands-on husband helped during the weekends. Their plan enabled him to stay alert at work.

Abi also planned to do her cooking over the weekend when her husband was available to help. She sometimes used the services of a local caterer to save her from cooking every weekend.

❋ Nola is married with two children, aged four and five. She worked full time, and because of the demands of her job, she employed a live-in nanny to help out with the children. Like Abi, she cooked in large quantities and froze these in smaller portions so her children can still enjoy her cooking while she was at work.

She also invested in a meal planner to make it easy for her to plan what meals to cook for her children. The meal planner also helped the live-in- nanny to know what food to heat up.

She planned to always video call her children from work after school. Her husband, who worked away from home on Mondays to Fridays, also did the same.

Nola also planned to take her annual leave from work during the children's school holidays, to make up for the lost time. She hardly attended social events over the weekends, especially those that restrict the attendance of children. She understands that being a mum to young children is only for a season, but her time now is for her family.

Action Plan

- Spend time praying to God. Ask Him to know the plans He has for you, your child and your parenting journey.

- Write down a monthly parenting goal. Make sure it is simple and achievable. You can also write down a goal for your child.

- Set a time daily to talk, listen and even read to your child. You can start at 15 minutes at least. Try as much as possible to pay attention to whatever they say and be genuinely interested. This time devoted to them reduces how often they would distract you just to get your attention. If your child is a baby, you can read and talk to them as this would get them used to the undivided attention from mum.

- Plan an activity with your child this week. The planned activity is an opportunity to bond, and it does not necessarily have to be expensive. You can plan to go for a walk or a drive and simply talk about the things you see as you go along.

- Write down the activities that get you stressed and look for ways to reduce the stress you experience. For instance, if getting the children ready in the morning is a pain, you can get their clothes and lunch boxes ready the night before.

✿ Create a menu plan for your child and your entire family. Menu plans can cover two weeks, with a set time for main meals and time for healthy snacks in between.

✿ Plan to have 'me' time at least 30 minutes daily. It is time to relax and unwind from the pressures of the day. You could soak yourself in the bathtub, have a shower, go for a short walk or listen to soft music.

✿ Get a notebook, diary or planner to write down your daily and weekly plans.

Personal Notes

Chapter
Two

Let all things be done decently and in order
1 Corinthians 14:40 (KJV)

Have a Routine

Since becoming a mother by God's grace and mercy alone, I have learnt to develop workable family routines that provide some level of order in our home. I choose to attribute this to my God-given organisation skills.

Before motherhood, I loved to arrange, plan and organise "anything and everything". I remember growing up as a young girl and spending my entire Saturday (every Saturday) cleaning the house, handwashing clothes, arranging my closet and bedside drawer and planning for the week ahead.

I can still remember singing at the top of my voice while I enjoyed these chores. Although the housekeeper did her bit and the washing machine did its bit, I made sure I did my large chunk too, and I enjoyed it.

Once blessed with a child, I put my skills to use. At the time, it was just another need to organise or clean "something". Little did I know that I was paving the way to stress-free motherhood.

Setting and planning daily routines was a crucial part of my achieving some form of order in my early years of parenting. I had routines for my daily tasks, from morning through to bedtime. I couldn't control the unpredictable nature of my baby, but I was bent on taking charge of how I used and spent my time to stop myself from getting burnt out. And honestly, routines saved the day.

Daily routines help to structure time, provide order and make the early parenting years a lot manageable. So what are routines?

Routines are a sequence of actions followed regularly. It is a common set of activities that are undertaken at a given time or period. It can also be an order of events carried out to complete a task. For instance, having a shower before going to bed daily, taking your child for football practice every Saturday or going to the hairdresser once a month, are all forms of routines.

The Bible speaks of Jesus Christ and his routine in Luke Chapter 4 verse 16:

So He came to Nazareth, where He had been brought up. And as His custom was, He went into the synagogue on the Sabbath day and stood up to read. - Luke 4:16 (NKJV)

This was also the case with Daniel in Daniel Chapter 6 verse 10:

Chapter Two

Now when Daniel knew that the writing was signed, he went home. And in his upper room, with his windows open toward Jerusalem, he knelt down on his knees three times that day, and prayed and gave thanks before his God, as was his custom since early days. - Daniel 6:10 (NKJV)

The above scriptures indicate that there should be some practices in our lives described as our custom, tradition or routine.

Do you have any routines? Are there any practices that people would describe as your routines? Can this be translated to your parenting? Fear not and fret not if you haven't got any routine in place. I do pray this chapter will give you the necessary titbits required to set your routine.

Routines contribute to the achievement of plans. For instance, you may plan to go to the gym every Wednesday night, but if you fail to go, the plan remains just that, a lovely plan. However, when you consistently go to the gym over a long period, it then becomes a routine.

Interestingly, not all plans become routines. Some are for one-off occasions. Although you may win the mum-of-the-year award for taking your child to a theme park every weekend, it will undoubtedly cause physical, mental and most likely financial strain.

Routines aim to minimise the pressures faced and create order when parenting our children. Simply put, routines produce order, order result in better use of time, and this invariably leads to higher levels of productivity. With more time on our hands, we can unwind from the daily pressures and give our best to our children.

The benefits of routines are not exclusive to mothers. Our children benefit from the establishment of routines because it provides them with a sense of security. Children tend to behave better because the structure of routines assures them of what to expect. Children are less likely to feel frustrated and upset over every little thing if they know what to expect most of the time.

Fewer behavioural problems occur when the household operates in a way that allows for consistency and routines. For instance, a child with no established bedtime routine would always kick a fuss when asked to go to bed. They tend to go to bed rather late and with less amount of sleep, wake up tired and grumpy in the morning, which already introduces stress for the mother first thing in the day.

Another benefit of routines is that it teaches children the importance of organisation. Children are likely to continue with the routines they grew up with, without being prompted. For example, a child that always brushes their teeth before going to bed will most likely continue this routine until old age (except they just can't be bothered about their hygiene).

Although routines help to alleviate the pressure of the unknown, a bit of spontaneity should be encouraged. From experience, I noticed my children were more open to doing what they were asked as long as it was within the boundaries of our family routine, and it did not come as a shock to them. However, when there was a change in routine, they questioned the change and had to be persuaded and convinced with salient points.

I quickly learnt that my children would respond positively to change if they were informed beforehand. For instance, when they were younger, and I had to arrange for childcare during the weekends, I made sure they were aware in advance. On such occasions, I found that they were more receptive of my absence, and it drastically reduced the likelihood of tears and tantrums when I left home.

Our routines need to be practical, consistent and realistic. Once set, we need to keep at it. It should not be a case of here today and gone tomorrow. Setting routines should be pressure-free and introduced gradually.

Life and motherhood will be boring if it is rudimental and overly structured; however, routines will help ease the day to day structure. Routines must also meet our needs. Just because the lady next door has time for every activity on planet Earth, does not mean we can and should take on much more than we can handle. Copying another's style might defeat the purpose of easing stress and mount the pressure of motherhood.

Furthermore, routines will need to be adjusted to accommodate life's changes, such as growth. Bedtimes routines, morning routines and mealtime routines will change as our children get older.

Before the initiation of any routine, the following three questions should be asked and answered: -

What are my daily activities?

What activities can be designated at the same time every day?

Which of these can I do consistently?

Once the above questions have been answered, a set time and set tasks can be assigned to each activity.

Another way to set routines is by assigning a day for each household chore. It is particularly useful when children are

---

young, and there are no extra hands to help out. Please see an example below.

Monday – Cleaning (house)
Tuesday – Laundry
Wednesday – Cleaning (kitchen/toilets)
Thursday – Shopping (Online shopping preferably)
Friday – Laundry
Saturday – Bulk cooking
Sunday – Church/Rest

Set routines will differ from one mum to the next, and it should reflect each one's needs. The benefits of having a home where everyone works within a realistic routine are innumerable. It is well worth the effort.

What Some Mums Did

 For Juliet, routines helped to ease the pressures of being a single mum caring for two young children. Once her children slept through the night, she ensured they went to bed at 8 pm. She had a bedtime routine where her children brushed their teeth, washed their faces, enjoyed a bedtime story and said their prayers daily.

Although it was initially difficult, Juliet made sure it became a consistent practice. Once the children were in bed, Juliet used the time to catch up on household chores, prepare for the next day, read a book or just relax in front of the TV.

 To give herself time to rest after the birth of her new baby, Abi had a routine in place for her household chores. Her routines strictly consisted of completing set tasks on specific days. She also fed her baby at regular planned intervals to give her time in between meals to tend to other affairs on her to-do list or to simply sleep once her baby was fast asleep.

 For Nola, her life revolved around routines. She woke up at 5 am every working day and had a lie-in on Saturdays. Due to her busy schedule at work, she set up a routine for her children's live-in nanny to follow. She set up this structure

to ensure that whenever there is a change in nanny, her children would still have their routine in place.

Nola also ensured that wake up time, bedtimes and mealtimes are at set times during weekdays, and she allowed some flexibility at weekends when she relieved the nanny.

Nola had a routine for her Christian life. She had her quiet time at night. It consisted of reading the Bible and prayers for her needs and the needs of others.

Action Plan

Establish a morning routine. It should include a set time to get out of bed. Ensure this is done at the same time every day. Set times can be different at weekends when there may be more time on your hands.

Set out routines for house chores. List out the various activities you do each week and allocate days for each one that best suits you. For example, you can clean on Saturday mornings; and complete household shopping online on a set day.

Prepare for the morning the night before. Put out and iron clothes for the next day, prepare the children's lunch boxes the night before and store in the refrigerator.

Teach the children to do chores by associating it with a routine. For instance, children can tidy up their toys before listening to stories at bedtime. They can also put their dirty clothes in the laundry basket before dinner. This seemingly little acts can help alleviate stress.

Sleep at the same time every day.

Try to get up ten minutes earlier in the mornings as it allows you to cope with any unpredictable incidence.

Personal Notes

Chapter Three

Give instruction to a wise man and he will be wiser: teach a just man, and he will increase in learning.
Proverbs 9:9 (KJV)

Establish Clear Boundaries

Establishing boundaries is another way to cope better with the stress on our parenting journey. Our stress levels are usually on the rise when dealing with situations where our children fall short of our expectations of them. Stress levels also increase during periods of discipline or correction, especially when we want our children to do as we say. We get worked up when they fail to follow our instructions; however, the dip and rise of our stress levels can be managed with clear boundaries.

Clear boundaries limit undesirable behaviour. Without boundaries, all deeds, good or bad, will be permissible. Without it, adults and children can freely run riot; no rules would be broken because there was none in the first place.

An excellent example of boundary setting can be described using the scenario of the child, the fireguard and the fireplace. The fireguard is a metal frame placed in front of the fireplace to prevent the child from burning themselves or from playing with open fire. In this scenario, the fireguard represents the boundaries set to encourage acceptable behaviour or actions from the child. The fireplace, on the other hand, represents the consequences the child will face when there are no boundaries (fireguard) in place.

Chapter Three

So then, what are boundaries? I chose to define this as the line drawn between what is acceptable and what is not. Boundaries are synonymous to walls, borders, laws, gates, limits, rules, regulations, restrictions and also margins. Everyone must have set boundaries that guide daily actions.

Like a city that is broken without walls (leaving it unprotected) is a man who has no self-control over his spirit (and sets himself up for trouble) - Proverbs 25:28 (AMP)

The above Bible verse talks about a man with no self-control, but then I thought, how will you describe a person, child or adult if they had no self-control? How will you describe them if they had no principles to guide their behaviour? As harsh as it may sound, an adult or child brought up without limits or boundaries is like this city without walls.

A city without walls will welcome anything and anyone. Lawlessness will be the standard practice in such a city. Chaos will be the order of the day. Without set boundaries, everyone will feel justified to do as they please.

Lack of boundaries will leave children unprotected and prone to trouble, and this will only leave Mummy dearest, stressed out and burnt out.

Boundaries for our children can be verbal and non-verbal. Non-verbal boundaries comprise of objects or items put in place to prevent harm like the fireguard and stair gates which prevent young children from falling down the stairs or from climbing up the stairs unsupervised. These are non-verbal boundaries that signify to the child at whatever age, that the stairs and the fireplace are out of bounds.

Clear boundaries help to clarify expectations. Setting boundaries focuses on how we can encourage our children to act acceptably (most times by God's grace). In this context, it is the boundary that separates good behaviour from unacceptable behaviour, which is relative.

Our view of what is acceptable or unacceptable depends on our foundation, background, culture, religion and society. However, I firmly believe that the Holy Bible should be our guide. Why? It is because kingdoms rise and kingdoms fall, governments change, laws are reviewed, but the Word of God never changes. It is our only constant.

Don't suppose for a minute that I have come to demolish the Scriptures—either God's Law or the Prophets. I'm not here to demolish but to complete. I am going to put it all together, pull it all together in a vast panorama. God's Law is more real and lasting than the stars in the sky and the ground at your feet. Long after stars burn out and earth wears out, God's Law will be alive and working.
- Matthew 5:17-18 (MSG)

God's word should be our reference point for setting boundaries to guide our children on the straight and narrow path and to help us on our stress-free parenting journey.

Boundaries are put in place to protect and also produce acceptable behaviour. It helps to instil ethical values in children. The set boundaries should not create fear in the child, but it should be established in a way that will encourage the child to do right. The focus of setting boundaries is on the positive all wrapped up in loads of meaningful praise.

Children, including adults, respond better to positive statements, praise and encouragements rather than the negative. Setting boundaries does not guarantee obedience from children; however, approval and affirmation help to boost good behaviour. It is essential to focus on good behaviour rather than the bad. Praise children when they do right even when they are not aware you were watching.

While my children were a lot younger, I had a thing about them standing or jumping on the sofa. Honestly, I still can't stand it, so this was one of my set boundaries for my energetic boys. After I had spent the best part of my time complaining about their acrobatic skills on the sofa, I changed my tactics. Whenever I noticed they were sitting on the sofa, I praised them; I thanked them for listening and obeying instructions. They must have preferred 'this mum' to the ever complaining mum, and they stopped jumping on the sofa.

It is undoubtedly a mammoth task to remain positive amid so many daily demands. I remember a time I set boundaries or better still, rules and regulations as I went along the day. My vocabulary was dominated by "don't" and "stop" sentences. It became so obvious when I started working from home. I sounded like a broken record repeating "commandments" around the house. I knew I had to change after I heard my son complain to his dad, "Why is mum always shouting?"

"What? Me! Shout!" I spent the next couple of days listening to myself, and I did not like what I heard. I was becoming stressed while trying to instil discipline in my home. I realised that too many boundaries would cause resentment, leading to the children's continuous display of unacceptable behaviour.

I had to clearly distinguish between what I deemed important and behaviour I was willing to overlook. As the children got older, we agreed on some boundaries while some others were not debatable.

As impressive as it may sound, my boundaries worked better when everyone agreed to it. For instance, my boys could play and mess up their playroom, as long as it got tidied up at the end of the day, of course, with help from mum.

Chapter Three

It is vital to remain consistent when setting boundaries, so the children are not left confused. Dear mum, if you question an unacceptable behaviour on Monday, you should not condone it on Wednesday. In other words, remain constant and never send mixed messages to your child.

Most importantly, it would be a complete waste of time and energy if you stress yourself over naughty behaviour when the child is not aware of their actions. Imagine this scenario:-

Father to son: *"Why don't you listen to your mum?"*
Son: *"I do."*

Father: *"But she always complains that you touch her glass jar on the dining table."*

Son: *"Oh, no, Dad! She just complains about the flower vase close to the jar. I think she feels I'll break it, but I never touch it."*

Mum overhears their conversation and responds.

Mum: *"You've both got it wrong; I am concerned that our son would eat all the biscuits in the jar!"*

Father and son look confused.
Son and Father: *"Why didn't you just say so?!!"*

In the above scenario, the mum had been stressing over the biscuits in the jar; but this was not communicated to her son. To avoid being misunderstood, boundaries should be clear and easily understood by children.

What Some Mums Did

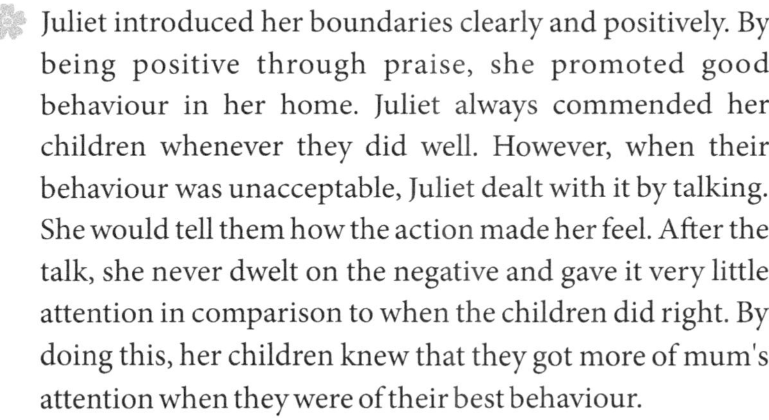

Juliet introduced her boundaries clearly and positively. By being positive through praise, she promoted good behaviour in her home. Juliet always commended her children whenever they did well. However, when their behaviour was unacceptable, Juliet dealt with it by talking. She would tell them how the action made her feel. After the talk, she never dwelt on the negative and gave it very little attention in comparison to when the children did right. By doing this, her children knew that they got more of mum's attention when they were of their best behaviour.

Lade, a stay at home mum of a three-year-old, also managed her daughter's behaviour through praise and words of encouragement. Each time her daughter used a polite word; Lade acknowledged this and praised her. However, when her child exhibited unacceptable behaviour, there were consequences in place. These included taking away a favourite toy or reducing screen time on a device or in front of the TV.

On the other hand, Nola used different mechanisms to set boundaries. Time out was used to maintain good behaviour. It consisted of her children sitting in a corner or going up to their room for a set time.

Time out worked well for both the children and Nola. Time out separated the children from the situation that may have prompted the unacceptable behaviour and for Nola; it gave her time to calm down and stopped her from overreacting based on her emotions at the time.
Nola ensured that her children understood why their behaviour was unacceptable.

Apart from time out, Nola believed the saying that little drops of water make a mighty ocean; therefore, she nipped unacceptable behaviour in the bud immediately it reared its ugly head. For instance, if the children yelled at her, she corrected them quickly, highlighting the importance of respect in a calm manner. She hoped that the children would not repeat the act, but if they did, she would remind them of their previous conversation. If the behaviour persisted, time out was implemented.

The live-in nanny also followed the set household boundaries with guidance from Nola.

Action Plan

* Start giving meaningful praise to your children. Think about times when you have been praised and complimented for your actions. How did you feel? Did it motivate you to do more? Well, that is how praise affects children too.

* Set achievable boundaries. It may be as simple as insisting on being polite, asking your permission before taking things and tidying up after playing with toys. Your child must understand what is expected of them.

* For any particular "problem" behaviour, it is advisable to try the reward system. It can be in the form of a chart or sticker book. For each time the child does what they are told without a fuss, a star is rewarded, and a collection of five stars or more will result in a treat.

* Set limits for yourself; think about how you deal with unacceptable behaviour and what you could do better.

* Set consequences for unacceptable behaviour. Consequences should be age-appropriate. More importantly, it should be set from a place of love and not to punish your child.

Personal Notes

Chapter Four

*Death and life are in the
power of the tongue*
**Proverbs 18:21a
(KJV)**

Speak Life

As mothers, the words we speak to our children can either produce life or death. This may sound harsh, but our words can either lift or pull down. Spoken words have the power to build up or tear down. If we took note, we would realise that our spoken words fall into two categories or boxes as I prefer to call them; the good box and the bad box.

The good box consists of words that encourage, words that lift, words that give life and words that propel us to act right. On the other hand, the bad box consists of all the opposites; words that destroy and words that deflate. The bad box simply consists of negative words.

Speaking life is simply about using words that are positive when communicating with our children. I thought this was impossible until I attended a Childcare Course over 14 years ago. I remember how the tutor kept stressing that we focus on the positive and not the negative when speaking to children. I understood what she meant about positive reinforcement, but how was this to work in day to day life, I asked myself.

It was just as if she had read my mind, and immediately she went on to ask what we would do if a two-year-old child in our care drew on our newly painted white wall. Our facial expressions gave us away; however, she continued by asking the class what we would say or do.

At this point, we all forgot to raise our hands and quickly responded in a disorderly manner. Many screamed out angrily, "NO! Don't do that". Others said they'd grab the crayon from the child and a few said they'll complain to the parent. As for me, I would have done all of the above. Surprisingly enough, the tutor disagreed with all our answers. This was getting rather interesting. Once again, the tutor emphasised positive reinforcement through the words we speak and gave a few examples of what we could say as we lead the child away from the wall, such as:-

"Your picture would look nicer on this sheet of paper."
"Do colour in your book."
"Come and help me with this picture."

The tutor gave more examples, and then it all made perfect sense. I left the class that evening feeling enlightened; I had learnt something new about Childcare but most importantly, about speaking positively to my children.

I also got a better understanding of the scripture in Proverbs 18 verse 21:-

Chapter Four

Words kill, words give life; they're either poison or fruit – you choose.' - Proverbs 18:21 (MSG)

Now, how was I to do this?

How do I stop using negative words?

How do I de-programme myself from screaming, 'NO' all the time?

'This change was going to be a huge task', I thought as I journeyed home.

Speaking life does not come easy. It takes determination and a conscious effort. Taking each day at a time will do a whole world of good. It is a gradual process that requires us reflecting on the words we use when addressing our children. Remember the words used should produce positive behaviour which will save us from stress in the long run. Similarly, when negative words are used all the time, there should be no surprises when the child begins to display the words spoken.

There are circumstances when our children may act in ways that we feel justified as mums to use harsh words. Yes, I hear you say but pause and reflect on what the Word says in Romans 4 verse 17b:-

'God, who gives life to the dead and calls those things which do not exist as though they did'. - Romans 4:17b (NKJV)

It merely means that when we choose to speak life, we are calling into existence what we want to see. When we speak life, we call forth the character traits we desire in our children. When we speak life, we are creating our world just as God did in the beginning. Although it was dark everywhere, God said in Genesis 1 verse 3:-

'Let there be light and there was light'. -Genesis 1:3 (NKJV)

Like children of our heavenly Father, let us use our words to form our children and our world. Once there is a determination to speak life, it would be profitable when it is done all the time.

Apart from the fact that speaking life helps with the upbringing of children, it rubs off on us, the parents, as we begin to apply positive words to every situation that we face.

As we know, children are like sponges. They imitate what we say and do, which is a useful attribute when we want positive speaking to rub off on them.

I remember a few years ago when one of my sons was very upset because his friend had called him, "naughty". As harmless as it may sound, my children refuse to be addressed in such a manner. Even when I accidentally use the word, I am quickly corrected by one of them. Indeed a child's action can be described as naughty but not the child.

An easy strategy which embeds positive words in our language is the use of key phrases as a reminder of speaking life. I formed some of these in my early parenting days which were of tremendous help to me on this journey. Some of my positive phrases included:-

* You are a good boy, so what do good boys do?

* Please act like the good boy that you are.

* Please walk nicely.

* Use your kind words.

* Let's use our indoor voice.

* Is that a good way to speak to mummy?

You could make up phrases based on personal choice; however, the emphasis must be on the positive and not the negative. I must say, I did slip (and still do slip), and as earlier mentioned, my children would draw my attention to it.

Each time I spoke contrary words, I would apologise to my children and God. I would be so hard on myself and think up more ways to cope until I realised that there was nothing I could achieve "permanently" in my strength.

As I delved deeper into God's word, I understood that I needed more of Him in me. I needed to believe in His power to overcome negative speaking. I realised that if I continually trusted in Him and His power, then rivers of life will flow freely from within me as stated in John 7 verse 38:-

'Whoever believes in me, as scripture has said, rivers of living water will flow from within them'. - John 7:38 (NIV)

In other words, although strategies do help, a sustained change comes from spending time in His Word and believing in Him. As we grow in Him, we begin to speak words that will shape our world.

Speaking life extends to everything that pertains to us as mothers. Positive words are needed to frame and make our day. The dawn of each day cries for words of life. Words declaring that:-

✳ Today is going to be a great day.

✳ I have the strength to succeed in all my endeavours today.

🌸 My children will be their best today.

🌸 Favour, grace and mercy are mine today.

🌸 We will go out in peace and return home in peace.

🌸 I will rejoice and be glad in this day.

Speaking positive words ensures children see the world from a positive viewpoint. Positive children believe in themselves. A child may have problems doing up their buttons or lacing up their shoes, but when they are told that they can do it, they soon accomplish the task due to the resounding words of affirmation.

This analogy also extends to behavioural issues. When a child who has begun to play up is constantly told that they can do better, will over time, begin to change. The timing of change surely differs from child to child, but it does happen if we keep at it and are consistent.

It is crucial that we get things right, now, not tomorrow but now. Once the words of life can cause our children to act right, it will surely reduce the stress of constant reprimanding thereby giving us one less thing to worry about on our parenting journey.

What Some Mums Did

✻ Juliet, the single mum of two, considered positive words a significant part of her children's upbringing. She believed that using positive words throughout their childhood would lay the foundation of self-belief and high self-esteem.

Juliet believed that if lots of positive words do not surround children at a tender age, they could rely on vices for affirmation. The phrases "I love you" and "You are the best" were a constant in her vocabulary.

✻ Lade was also a firm believer in providing a positive environment for her toddler. To derive good behaviour from her toddler, she asked questions like, "Are you a princess?" Once there was an affirmative response, Lade would say, "Then please act like a princess". Positive words are part of her way of life, and she used it not only to achieve good behaviour or become stress-free but to build up her child.

Lade also had affirmation cards written out to recite to her daughter, in the morning and at night time. The reading of affirmation cards became a routine, and her daughter would always remind her to read the cards if she forgot to peak 'the words of life'.

 While Nola tried to achieve the perfect work-life balance, she managed to speak words of life whenever she got the chance to. Before she rushed off in the morning, she blessed her children with words of life and prayers. She declared that they would always be the head, always be the best and inevitably be the greatest. These words had become a cliché, and the children recited it to themselves.

At other times, Nola used the phrases to guide her children back to acceptable behaviour; for instance, she would say, "Remember you are the best". Nola also used affirmation cards and positive confessions to speak life to herself.

Action Plan

* Spend time in God's word. The more you read or listen to His word, the more you sound like Him.

* Start your day with God, and commit your struggles and your words to Him.

* Listen out for the words and tone you use when addressing your children. Make a note of the negative and please eliminate it.

* Learn to keep quiet when stressed or upset. This would prevent you from saying negative words.

* Learn to walk away or ignore the situation until you know you are in control of your emotions and words. Counting to 10 is an excellent way to manage your emotions when upset, but if you are like me, I suggest counting to 50 or repeating the lines, 'Our Father who hath in Heaven, hallowed be Your name' ten times.

* Be quick to apologise to your children when you speak negative words to them. Also, pray to God that the negative words spoken to them will not come to life.

* Write out three positive phrases and use them daily. You

can begin by using these phrases at a particular time of the day; bedtime or when leaving home in the morning.

❋ Make up a positive phrase to handle inappropriate behaviour. Remember, practice makes perfect.

Personal Notes

Chapter Five

Choose life,
that both thou and
thy seed will live.
Deuteronomy 30:19b
(King James Version)

Live
Life

Dear mums, let us pause to thank God for the gift of life. Without His grace and mercy, we would not be here today. Psalm 124 is a good reminder of how God continually saves us in the face of attacks which may be known or unknown to us.

What if God had not been on our side? Let all Israel admit this! What if God had not been there for us? Our enemies, in their violent anger, would have swallowed us up alive! The nations, with their flood of rage, would have swept us away and we would have drowned, perished beneath their torrent of terror! We can praise God over and over that he never left us! God wouldn't allow the terror of our enemies to defeat us. We are free from the hunter's trap; their snare is broken and we have escaped! For the same God who made everything, our Creator and our mighty maker, he himself is our helper and defender! - Psalm 124 (TPT)

If not for God, we will not be here today to nurture the great children He has given us. Once again, take some time to thank Him for the privilege of motherhood.

As mums, we expend a lot of our energy on parenting and nurturing our children without spending time on ourselves.

We make time for everyone else but neglect to care and pamper number one - ourselves. Many of us have forgotten or let go of the activities we used to enjoy before we became mothers. This should not be the case.

Being a mum is a never-ending role that requires time and energy; however, it is vital that we spend some time on ourselves, to recoup, refresh, and be revitalised, after all, no one can pour from an empty cup.

So dear Stress Free Mum, before you run out of energy, take some time to take care of you by living your life. To live life is to enjoy living. It is to live and do the things we love despite being a mother. Living life can be achieved when we set aside some time to treat ourselves after a hard day or week and please - no 'mummy-guilt' feeling is allowed.

Ecclesiastes Chapter 3 verses 1 to 4 reminds us that there is time for everything,

There is a time for everything, and a season for every activity under the heavens: a time to be born and a time to die, a time to plant and a time to uproot, a time to kill and a time to heal, a time to tear down and a time to build, a time to weep and a time to laugh, a time to mourn and a time to dance,
- Ecclesiastes 3:1-4 (NIV)

We should set time aside to heal and build ourselves up after being exasperated from parenting. We can use those times to enjoy leisure activities, a hobby, or just being on our own. Motherhood should not be the reason why we stop living our lives.

Over the years, I have seen and heard many mothers blame their children for their underachievement as they call it. Indeed, a woman filled with so much resentment would be stressed and incapable of giving her best to her children. However, once we create time to enjoy the things we love, our children will never be held responsible for our supposed failure to live life.

According to experts, doing what we enjoy for ourselves can help boost our ability to recover from stress. Finding that time for ourselves is not as hard as we may think. Extra time can be found by waking up a little earlier or through better time management and planning. Through the help of God, I have managed to have time for myself by setting routines and by planning (Chapter One & Two).

My established bedtime routine was strictly followed, and with the children in bed at 7:30 pm, I had the remaining time to use wisely. Depending on my day, I sometimes had an early night, but if I still had the energy to keep going, I used the time to finish up leftover tasks around the house, write or start a job planned for the following day. I sometimes pampered myself by having a bubble bath, soaking my feet in a bucket of warm water, listening to music or reading a book. I choose to call this my "me time".

I do have "me time" every day, even given my other responsibilities such as being a wife, a sister, a daughter, an employee, a business owner, a friend and a co-pastor. Given my varied roles, the "me time" helps to keep me refreshed and recharged. Daily time spent on me varies from as little as 30 minutes to as much as an hour.

As mothers, it is crucial to set time aside on a daily, weekly, monthly and yearly basis, depending on what we opt for. Setting time aside is just a way to plan for relaxing activities that will help ease our stress after a busy day or period. The purpose of "me time" is to get rejuvenated when we engage in activities that are relaxing and fulfilling. For example, we could read a book, learn a new language, start exercising, go for walks, sit outside for some fresh air, have a shower, soak ourselves in a bath or simply go to bed. It is certainly not an avenue to condone idleness because apart from recouping or unwinding, we can use the time towards self-improvement.

Dear Stress Free Mum, it is time to start living. It is time to enjoy who we are while nurturing our seeds of greatness. Our role as mothers should not and cannot limit us. With a little thought, planning, time management and determination, we can surely create some time for ourselves which will be another step away from a stressful life.

What Some Mums Did

❁ Juliet often got stressed because she had to juggle between the roles of mum and dad; thus, she had her "me time" every day. During lunchtime at work, she would go out for a stroll just to be by herself.

At home, once the children were in bed, she invested about an hour on herself. She often read books to improve her skills as she prepares for her professional exams. She refused to blame her single parenthood for her lack of career progression, and she made every effort to achieve this.

On other times, Juliet had her "me time" by having long showers and meditating on God's word.

❁ Abi has her "me time" during the day when her baby is fast asleep. She usually has a nap when physically tired, and when she feels up to it, she exercises to get back in shape after pregnancy. She also has some time to herself on Saturdays when her husband assists with the baby.

❁ Nola hardly had time for herself due to the pressure from work, and so she had her "me time" when she drove home after a long day at work. She listened to her favourite music as she endured the city's traffic. Once she arrived home, she sat alone in the car for a few minutes. Nola used the time to consciously switch off from her role as Company Manager to that of wife and mother.

As part of her "me time" plan, Nola attended an annual spa retreat. She did this in agreement and support of her husband. The retreat was a time when she shut out the whole world to gain strength for the journey ahead. Sometimes, Nola had a retreat at home where she spent at least 6 hours in a room with no TV, laptop or mobile phone. She called this her time of refreshing. She planned to do this every quarter, again with the support and help of her husband.

Action Plan

- Set aside at least 30 minutes a day to do whatever you please.

- Go for a stroll alone.

- Go to bed early even before you feel sleepy.

- Wake up a little earlier.

- Have a relaxing bath or shower regularly.

- Start a hobby.

- Start reading quality books.

- During "me time", turn off the TV and your phone.

- Think of something you would like to do for yourself and try to incorporate it into your "me time".

- Start thinking about ways to improve yourself – academically, physically, socially and spiritually

- Plan to go on a retreat or break, at least once a year

- Please write your structured plan down lest you forget

Personal Notes

Chapter Six

*A good name is more
desirable than great riches;
to be esteemed is better
than silver or gold.*
**Proverbs 22:1
(NIV)**

Be a Role Model

As a pregnant woman, I prayed that my unborn child would have what I thought were my beautiful features and I strongly hoped that my husband's genes would complement the areas where I fell short, like my scanty eyebrows. I also had a list of character traits that I wanted my seed of greatness to possess. My child had to be smart, quiet natured, well behaved; love the things I love, and the list was endless. Little did I know that I had a significant role to play in the traits exhibited by my child, and my wish lists were just words. Yes, it would be mere words if I did nothing to make them a reality.

I tried my utmost best to mould this baby in my strength, but now I was faced with this twenty-year-old in the form of an 18-month-old. The word 'NO' had become his immediate response to any of my requests.

'How do I get my toddler to do what I want?' I thought as I struggled to teach him social etiquette. I had reached my wits end regarding the life lessons on being polite. Then I remembered the phrase that children are like sponges. They soak in whatever you do. Eureka! That was it. I decided to start practising what I preached.

Things moved from 'do as I say' to 'do as I do'. I had to become my son's role model. I had to be a person worth emulating. It was scary because there were some parts of me that I could not bear to see my child imitate. This motherhood thing wasn't as easy as I thought. It meant that I had to consciously work on myself before I could instil good values in my children. Well, they say the journey of a thousand miles begins with one step, and so my trip to reformation and transformation began.

Don't copy the behaviour and customs of this world, but let God transform you into a new person by changing the way you think. Then you will learn to know God's will for you, which is good and pleasing and perfect. - Romans 12:2 (NLT)

Although determined to make the change, I had to rely on God to change me from within. Being a good role model had to be according to God's standards and not the world's. If the world says it is okay, but it contradicts what God expects of us, then it's a no-no. We must understand the need to be good role models as parents, not just the mother. Children spend most of the foundation years with their parents, and it is the time when behaviours are formed. It is also a time when they learn from what they see around them, simply put, they reflect whatever we exhibit.

I remember an incident I witnessed between a mother and her son. Here goes: -

Chapter Six

Many years ago, I went shopping in a large superstore and experienced first-hand the importance of being a good role model. As I strolled through the aisle, a toddler was throwing a huge, no, a major tantrum. His mother tried to calm him, but it only worsened matters.

As he kicked and rolled on the shop floor, many other parents kept giving this already stressed-out mum, a disdainful look. I felt moved with 'selfish' compassion and prayed that my children would never do such. Unfortunately, things continued to go worse, and this handsome little boy resorted to using swear words. I was shocked and quickly walked past because I had heard enough. I carried on with my shopping still pondering on the shameful situation.

How can a two or three-year-old use such words? I thought as I paid for my shopping and proceeded away from the checkout counter, and then I noticed the mum and son again, but this time mum was in control. I was glad; however, this quickly changed to great disappointment when I heard the mother use the same swear words to buttress her point as she spoke to her son.

What! No wonder! Well, this apple surely did not fall far from the tree and had picked up the horrible words from his mother. What a shame!

We drop it, and our children pick it up – words, character traits, body languages and the list goes on and on. Hence we must ask – What do we say or do when our children are present or not?

Parents and especially mothers, should speak politely at all times, even to their children. Words like 'Please', 'Thank you', 'You are welcome' should be part of our daily vocabulary. When these words are used, we should not be surprised to see our very young children using the same words. There will be occasions when it may skip their minds, but by reminding and gently stressing the importance of being polite, it becomes part of them too.

I remember a time when I was busy in the kitchen, and I sneezed. Unknown to me, my then two-year-old heard, and he screamed from the other room, "Bless you, mummy". I was thrilled. I had not taught him to say that, but I guess he must have heard mum, dad or someone else say it. He was simply repeating what he had heard and seen. Thank God it was a good attribute.

I also noticed a time in my home when my children just loved to yell. Yelling was part of playtime, mealtime, bath time, everything. I became concerned but didn't have to look too far to discover what had gone wrong. Mum had lost it. I was just stressed and too selfish to deal with it. Then I realised that my children were only emulating mum's latest trait. By yelling, I unknowingly taught them to yell whenever they confronted stressful situations. I had to change.

Create in me a pure heart, O God, and renew a steadfast spirit within me. - Psalm 51:10 (NIV)

I needed a clean heart. I needed to be constant and dependable – not up today and down tomorrow. No amount of practice could do the trick, only the intervention of God's help. I had to change, and He had to create something new in me. I am still on my journey, and He continues to show me through His Word, areas of my life where change is required.

Apart from our words, it is crucial to be a role model in every other area. The following questions can help us assess our ways:-

❀ Do we tidy up after ourselves?

❀ What programmes do we watch when our children are present or not?

❀ What kind of songs do we listen to or play around the house?

❀ Do we read books or spend our time in front of the TV and

on devices?

Do we speak kindly of others?

Are our phone conversations positive or negative?

Do we speak the truth at all times?

Do we practice what we preach?

Do we apologise to our children when we wrong them?

We may think it is unnecessary to apologise; however, this kind act exposes our children to the reality that everyone makes mistakes, even mum.

By actively being a good role model, our children copy these good traits, giving us one less thing to worry about and saving us from a whole load of stress.

What Some Mums Did

❀ Juliet desired to be a good role model to her children, particularly in the area of academics. She always had a book to read. She had the television turned off during weekdays but on at weekends. It was her way to imbibe the reading culture in her children. With the TV off, Juliet left age-appropriate books around the house, and they were ever so eager to pick up a book, especially when they saw her reading one.

❀ Lade, the stay at home, focused on a healthy lifestyle. She always bought fruits and vegetables which accompany every meal. She ensured her fruit bowl was easily accessible to her toddler so she could help herself throughout the day.

Lade avoided buying unhealthy snacks, and although her toddler sometimes has sweets, it is usually few and far between.

❀ Apart from good manners, Nola was keen for her children to develop a sense of responsibility. Although she worked full time and had a live-in nanny, she assigned chores to everyone in her household, including herself. The children had simple tasks like sorting out the laundry, tidying up their rooms and clearing up the table after mealtimes.

They happily did these tasks because they have seen their mum carry out hers, effectively and efficiently.

Action Plan

- Use polite words at all times.

- Look for problem areas and devise a way to be a role model, for instance, if your toddler does not like to tidy up their toys; try joining in after you have instructed them to tidy up. They would, of course, emulate you over time, and tidy up time would be less of a struggle.

- Practice what you preach.

- Exhibit good conflict resolution skills with your children. Avoid shouting and listen to what they have to say too.

- Admit your mistakes.

- Always model good relationships. Pay particular attention to how you talk to people around you.

- Always ask yourself, "Am I worth emulating?" Make the necessary adjustments.

Chapter Six

Personal Notes

Chapter Seven

*Woman
behold thy son*
John 19:26b
(King James Version)

Be a Mother

I once heard a saying that all women could have children but not every woman who has a child is a mother. After a long hard thought, I agreed with the statement. It is quite easy to point our fingers at women who have abandoned their children or women who gave their children up for adoption, yet failing to recognise that the above phrase may include us too if care is not taken.

We could be classed in this category of women if we perform our motherly duties ineffectively. When we know the expectation of us as mothers and do it, success is guaranteed. Imagine starting a new role without a job description or person specification, and yet you are expected to perform to your utmost ability. I must say that you would be stressed from the anxiety of starting the role as well as from the sheer ignorance of not knowing what to expect. It will feel like being thrown in at the deep end and expected to swim when you do not know how to float in water.

It is the same with motherhood because the role does not come with a manual. We all start the role with no experience, and we are expected to do excellently well in it.
Many of us suffer and are stressed in this role because we are

oblivious as to what to do. The overwhelming feeling of uncertainty can be destructive.

The Bible says in Hosea 4:6:-

My people are destroyed for lack of knowledge. Because you have rejected knowledge, I also will reject you from being priest for Me; Because you have forgotten the law of your God, I also will forget your children. - Hosea 4:6 (NKJV)

Yes, lack of knowledge in any area of life can lead to destruction. In recent times, there have been debates about who qualifies to be a better mother, the stay at home mum or the career mum. In this book, the stay at home mum refers to the mother who stays home to care for her child, while the career mum is the mother who goes out to work, leaving her child in the care of another during this period.

Some support the notion that stay at home mums stand a better chance, while the opposing view opts for the career woman. I am on the fence on this one because having experienced both situations; none of these stands out. Being a stay at home mum does not make one better than a career mum. I firmly believe that the time effectively spent in the role of motherhood determines the performance levels. For instance, a stay at home mum who spends all day in front of the TV is no match to the career mum who consistently invests at least two hours on her children daily.

The crux of the matter is dependent on the quality of time and care given to our children and not the quantity of time we spend around them. And at this juncture, I choose to rest my case.

So then, who is a mother, and what does her role entail? A mother from A to Z:-

A – A mother **admonishes** her child. She **advises** her child on the right choices to make and no matter what, she is always **affectionate.**

B – A mother **bears** the burdens of her child. She **brightens** their day with lots of encouragement and meaningful praise. She even **bandages** bruises without any nursing qualification. She is **brave** before the child and hides her fears within.

C – A mother **cares** for her child. She **corrects** her child in love. She sometimes cries when they cry. She is ever ready to give her child **cuddles.**

D – A mother **defends** her child even in moments where she shouldn't, but none can blame her. She makes **decisions** with her child at the centre. Most times, her career and dreams take a back seat for the sake of her child (only for a season).

E – A mother **encourages** her child daily. She enables her child to be the best they can be. She **endures** difficult situations for the sake of her child and always endeavours to build her child's esteem.

F – A mother **fights** for her child in the place of prayer. She **fends** for her child. She feels the **fear** and does the 'parenting thing' anyway.

G – A mother **guides** her child along the right path. She **guards** them with her life and will give anything to make their life journey easy.

H – A mother is **hardworking.** She **holds** her child in her heart forever. She hugs her child for as long as she can. She is **happy** to go without for the sake of her child.

I – A mother **invites** her child into her space and is **impartial.** She is a positive **influence** on her child. She ensures her child imbibes good values.

J – A mother **juggles** between roles. She **jokes** around with the child and family. She never takes herself too seriously.

K – A mother **keeps** everything in order as best as she can. She is **kind** and loving.

L – A mother **loves** selflessly. She uses her words to **lift** her child. She **listens** to what her child says or does not say, because she **listens** with her heart.

M – A mother **mentors** her child before others do. She does not wait for the school or Sunday school teacher to teach her child. **Multitasking** is her greatest strength. She is a good **manager** of resources.

N – A mother **nurtures** and **nourishes** her child. She **notices** when they are down and when they need an extra cuddle.

O – A mother **organises** her home and makes it a haven for her child.

P – A mother **prays** for her child all the time. She ensures that she takes everything to God in prayer. She also gives meaningful **praise** whenever possible.

Q – A mother **questions** things that appear untoward in the life of her child.

R – A mother is **reliable** and **resourceful,** ensuring she provides adequately for her child, with or without the support of the child's father.

S – A mother **shields** and **shelters** her young. She acts like a

swan, looking calm on the outside but with a lot going on inside.

T – A mother **teaches** and **trains** up her child in the way to go.

U – A mother **understands.** Her child is free to discuss anything with her.

V – A mother **vows** to stand by her children no matter what.

W – A mother **watches** over her child like a hawk. Even while her child is asleep, she steals glimpses of her child in the middle of the night.

X – A mother is **xany** when it comes to anything to do with her child. She is overly energetic when she has enough excuse to give up.

Y – A mother **yearns** to see her child succeed.

Z – A mother is **zealous.** She spends a lot of time and energy in seeing her child's dream come true.

Honestly, a mother's role surpasses the letters in the alphabet. I do not intend to sound bias, but motherhood is the role that has all other professions rolled into it. Mothers are the cooks that prepare delicious meals; the nurses that tend to the scrapped knees and the teachers that help with the homework. They are also the judges that serve as the mediator between two quarrelling youngsters, and they are the number one fan that screams the loudest when their child plays in a game. What more can we say other than motherhood is an endless job profile.

There are several mothers in the Bible that we can learn from, for example, Hagar, the mother of Ishmael. From Genesis 21, verse 14, Hagar was homeless, yet it was her responsibility to provide water and bread for her son. The Bible states that:-

So Abraham rose early in the morning, and took bread and a skin of water; and putting it on her shoulder, he gave it and the boy to Hagar and sent her away. - Genesis 21:14 (NKJV)

A mother, like Hagar, will sometimes be faced with situations where she solely 'shoulders' the responsibility of providing for her child. She never gives up even amid storms.

And the water in the skin was used up, and she placed the boy under one of the shrubs - Genesis 21:15 (NKJV)

Even in lack, a mother will ensure she provides 'something' for her child. Although Hagar had no food or drink to give Ishmael, she gave him a covering which was protection. She tried to create some level of comfort in the midst of adversity.

This is what mothers do.'

Then she went and sat down across from him at a distance of about a bowshot; for she said to herself, "Let me not see the death of the boy." So she sat opposite him, lifted her voice and wept. - Genesis 21:16 (NKJV)

A mother never takes her eyes off her child no matter the distance between them. She never wants any evil to befall her child. A mother, like Hagar, intercedes on behalf of her child by crying out to God in prayer.

Then God opened her eyes, and she saw a well of water. And she went and filled the skin with water, and gave the lad a drink.- Genesis 21:19 (NKJV)

A mother looks out for her child first. Hagar ensured that her child drank water, although the Bible does record this, I want to believe that Hagar gave her son the water to drink first before thinking of herself.

But here lies the question; how do we manage stress while performing the "greatest" job on earth? Stress levels are controlled when we take each day at a time and also invest some time in our children. Time spent with our children can include helping out with school work, advising, encouraging and caring. This time dedicated to the children will ensure they feel loved. From experience, I have learnt that I get through to my children when they are happy. It becomes easier to teach them, correct them, establish boundaries and to get them to talk to me. When they are grumpy, it seems a struggle to achieve desired outcomes, thereby causing me more stress.

Another reason why children may become grumpy could be neglect. While undergoing another Childcare course, I learnt that neglect is a form of abuse. I realised that parents or mothers are guilty of this offence when no interest is paid to their children's dietary needs, hygiene and physical wellbeing.

Show me a child that looks unkempt and inadequately dressed, and I would show you a parent or carer that is guilty of negligence. If we can strive to do effectively in our roles, then we would have happier children and reduce stress significantly.

On a final note, it is our responsibility as mothers to nurture our children and not the job of the government, society, nannies, teachers and relatives. Dear Stress Free Mum, it is time for us to step up in our role for duty calls! Indeed mother, behold your child.

What Some Mums Did

❄ Juliet ensured she provided the necessities for her children. These included wearing the right clothing for the very unpredictable British weather. She made sure her children got their feet measured every school holiday so that their shoes fit perfectly all year round.

She also ensured that her children ate healthy meals. The healthy meals helped to reduce the occurrence of illnesses, and this gave her one less thing to worry about.

❄ Lade, on the other hand, saw communication as a tool to express motherly love. Once her three-year-old got back from school, she gave her child her undivided attention. She did this with the TV turned off. She also stayed away from social media until her child was in bed. This allowed Lade to know more about her child. Her child felt loved, and it created an opportunity for Lade to manage unwanted behaviour. With such attention, her child gave her a breather when required.

❄ Before Nola started full-time work, she stayed at home with her children. However, it was when she returned to work that she realised she had not adequately invested time in her children. Although she was present physically, she was emotionally absent. Due to this shocking realisation, Nola determined to make changes. What did she do wrong?

As a stay at home mum, Nola spent her time doing whatever caught her attention. She woke up each day with no desire to achieve any goal while she left her children in front of the TV. Her wakeup call began when she returned to work, and her live-in nanny began to mention milestones her children had reached which Nola never noticed. She regretted the wasted time and became determined to become a better mother.

Action Plan

- List four attributes of a good mother according to your definition and see if you practice them. Ensure you imbibe it through planning.

- Whenever you are out and about, watch out for mother/child relationships, and glean the positive aspects from these.

- Give your children undivided attention daily from as little as 15 minutes.

- Write down three good things you already do with your children and build upon it.

- Ask your spouse or trusted friend what they admire most about your mother/child relationship. You may never have noticed the good things you do with your children.

Personal Notes

Chapter
Eight

*Master, I beseech thee,
look upon my son: for
he is mine only child.*
**Luke 9:38b
(KJV)**

Confident Childcare

One of the greatest stress relievers for mums with young children is an extra helping hand. The need for additional help is usually as a result of well-desired respite or simply just to accommodate a work-life balance. With the increasing number of women having to return to work to pay the bills, the search for alternative care for young children is also on the rise. Even when we find a suitable option for our children, we need to be convinced that our children will be well looked after.

No mother desires to spend her day at work, worrying about the safety and wellbeing of her child. Without this inner peace, there is a tendency to remain in perpetual worry and stress. Leaving our children with a childcare provider is bad enough; however, to leave them with an incompetent carer is worse.

As suitable adults, the chances of us knowingly consulting an inexperienced doctor are non-existent. Then why would we leave our children in the hands of an incompetent carer?

Looking for the best form of care begins with planning. Although this is not foolproof, it helps to prepare, giving you time to research the type of care that best suits your lifestyle and your child. The plan should also include the inherent needs of your child.

It will be sad to take a child comfortable with one-on-one care and place them suddenly in a large nursery setting. Although settling in periods are designed to help the child adjust, some children would not bulge no matter how long these last for.

These are some of the factors we need to take into account when choosing childcare. A parent with an unsettled child in any setting would undoubtedly be unsettled as well. It is crucial that you look out for what makes your child happy, and run with it.

There are different forms of childcare which fall into two major categories; care that takes place in the child's home, such as nannies, house helps, au pairs etc., and care that takes place outside the child's home such as childminders, nurseries, daycare centres, crèches and so on.

Given the differences in structure, all the forms of childcare have advantages and disadvantages. These need to be noted during the period of planning before selecting the best option. I have tried most of the forms of care from relatives (grandmas), to childminders, to nurseries, to au pairs and finally myself, and I must say that personally, nothing beats looking after my child myself.

It is not the type of childcare provided that is most important but the quality of care given. Mums who cannot afford to stay home with their children should be assured that the other forms of care have lots of benefits too.

Another consideration for choosing a type of childcare will depend on the cost. Stress becomes unavoidable when financial burdens are prevalent because of an expensive choice of childcare. Although good quality childcare is never cheap, our children do not need to go to the most costly provision. Remember, it is the quality of care that matters and not the cost of care.

It is also essential to look for a childcare provider that shares your beliefs or values. Sharing similar values as the childcare provider helps to create an avenue for the continuity of care; from the home to the childcare setting.

This point reminded me of the story of Moses in the Bible when his sister insisted that Pharaoh's daughter got a carer that will maintain the tradition, beliefs and values of baby Moses.

Then his sister said to Pharaoh's daughter, "Shall I go and call a nurse for you from the Hebrew women, that she may nurse the child for you?"8 And Pharaoh's daughter said to her, "Go." So the maiden went and called the child's mother.
- Exodus 2:7-8 (NKJV)

In my case, I remember quite well how I focused on the experience of the carer when looking for childcare; however, when I became a qualified Early Years Professional, I understood the importance of maintaining family practices, traditions and beliefs.

Furthermore, if you feel uncomfortable with the childcare, then it should not be an option for you. Trust your gut instinct, as long as you are sure it is not mere suspicion.

Before concluding with the childcare provider, ask questions to clarify any doubts. Below are a few questions you can ask during your initial visit to the childcare provider.

- How long have they been caring for children?

- Do they have any qualifications within childcare?

- How would they handle challenging behaviour?

- What policies do they have in place (e.g. Health and safety, Safeguarding children, Behaviour management, etc.)?

- How is their service monitored by the regulatory body or government?

- What activities do they plan for the children?

❀ How many children are in their care?

❀ Have they ever had any complaint?

❀ How was this handled?

Confident childcare can also include a trusted friend, neighbour or relative. As an always busy mum with young children, I sometimes arranged with friends to watch over my children for a few hours, especially at the weekends. The free time provided me with time to rest and my children time to socialise with their friends.

I firmly believe mums must have people around them to help out with care when needed. It should be reciprocal. For all we know, a few hours of sleep may just do the trick to alleviate stress.

What Some Mums Did

❄ Juliet used the services of the local day nursery to provide care for her children when she was at work. She felt assured that her children are well looked after by professionals. She believed that day nurseries would offer a continuity of care as her children grew up.

For her, the day nursery is the place for her children to socialise. There is also regular and stable care as staff absences do not affect the provision of care that her children receive. According to Juliet, nurseries offer a structured environment which aids the children's transition into school. Although the children may lack the one-on-one attention, and the fees may be quite expensive, Juliet preferred day nurseries because it best suits her current family situation.

❄ Although currently at home, Lade preferred her three-year-old to learn and play in a structured setting and so she attended a day nursery too. Lade believed that interacting with other children would boost her child's self-confidence. She is also of the opinion that the curriculum would include a whole range of activities that help to develop various skills in her child.

❄ Abi loved being a stay-at-home mum to her baby. She saw

the time as an investment that would surely outlive her. She got to nurture and care for her child personally. She believed that her time at home had reduced her stress levels because there is no struggle to maintain a work-life balance. Although staying at home allowed Abi to spend more time with her child and family, she sometimes felt lonely.

 Nola had a live-in nanny to care for her two children. According to her, the presence of a live-in nanny took the pressure off everyday family life. She also preferred having a nanny because it best suits her unpredictable work hours. She felt at ease, knowing that her children were cared for at home.

Although this was Nola's preference, she sometimes found it uncomfortable because she had to share her home with another adult.

Action Plan

* Look at your current childcare arrangement and assess if it helps relieve you of stress or contributes to it.

* If you are still searching for childcare, list the pros and cons of the care available to you before you make up your mind.

* If you feel unsure, visit the childcare provider at two different times of the day to get a full picture of how it runs.

* Prepare questions to ask during your visit.

* Ensure the childcare provider has the qualifications to care for children and has some level of experience.

* Look out for a clean, safe and child-friendly environment.

* Have a trusted friend who can help you with childcare for a few hours a month. Remember to be willing to reciprocate this kind gesture.

Personal Notes

Chapter
Nine

*Let us lay aside every
weight, and the sin which
doth so easily beset us*
Hebrews 12:1
(KJV)

Drop the Weights

I had intended to call this chapter "lose the weight", but chose not to put anyone off, especially myself. It reminds me of the different times I had tried, very hard, to shed a bit of weight. I must emphasise here that no one complained about the extra pounds I had put on over the years, but I was merely tired. I was tired of having to squeeze into a size 12 outfit when in fact I was verging on a size 14. It was indeed time for me to drop the weight.

I remember another time when I had gained a lot of weight due to my constant trips to the cake shop. My clothes did not fit anymore; I felt heavy and bloated and unfortunately could not run around the house with my children because I was always tired. After a lot of struggle, I decided to shed some weight; to drop the bad habits that were responsible for the extra pounds and flab.

So what has weight loss got to do with motherhood and de-stressing?

This chapter is not about a trip to the gym or a brisk walk around the park. It certainly isn't a ploy to get mothers to exercise, although that would not be a bad idea. It certainly isn't about our daily calorie intake and how to fit into a dress, one size down. Similar to the weight we sometimes pile on, there are weights in the form of habits that hinder our effectiveness as mothers. These weights prevent us from being our best to ourselves and our children.

These could be habits or situations that have weighed us down and have began to interfere with the relationship with our children and have taken priority over them. These weights include endless hours on the phone, sitting for hours in front of the TV, attending too many social events, and so on.

For the purpose of this chapter, let's call the weights the 'too much or too many syndromes', that is, too much TV, too many phone calls, too much talking, too much sleep, too much shopping, too much idleness, too many social activities, too many house chores, too many hours spent at work, and just doing too much at the detriment of fostering a healthy relationship with our children.

By getting rid of these habits which can also be called time stealers, we would have more time to ourselves, more time for our children and even a lot more time to rest and get rid of stress.

Imagine being sat on the phone for hours on end, chatting with the same friend you spoke to, the day before. The children are

Chapter Nine

still awake and haven't had dinner. By the end of the conversation, you then realise you barely have 30 minutes to cook a meal, feed them, do the dishes and then get them to bed. Undoubtedly, your stress levels would hit the roof.

Also, imagine you have the necessary childcare in place, and so you decide to honour another party invitation - this being the sixth party-filled weekend in a row. As exciting as this may sound, the hours spent at some of these social gatherings should be invested in our children. No one has ever gotten arrested for missing a party. The time can be used to get to know our children better, to bond and indeed love. Time with our children can never be overemphasised because it is such memories that they would hold onto.

The reduction of social events attended is not a call for unsociable mothers to arise but a cry for mothers to spend more quality time with their children. Social activities are enjoyable; keeping in touch with friends that build us up is also fun but not at the expense of building a healthy relationship with our children.

When we spend time with our children, we notice their good and bad habits, and we are quick to nip unacceptable behaviour in the bud before it becomes full-blown. Dealing with such traits instantly spares us the stress of having to manage the situation when it is way out of control.

Furthermore, when we spend more time with our children, we can instil good values in them. They also get to know us better. Also, the effort expended to set boundaries and establish routines would become wasted if we are not present to ensure these are well embedded.

To the mum who may be reading this and you are concerned that motherhood will 'cramp your style', please remember these words,

There is a time for everything, and a season for every activity under the heavens: a time to be born and a time to die, a time to plant and a time to uproot, a time to kill and a time to heal, a time to tear down and a time to build, a time to weep and a time to laugh, a time to mourn and a time to dance,
- Ecclesiastes 3: 1-4 (NIV)

It is clear from the above verses that there is time for every activity. It will be foolishness to try to do everything at the same time, and that is where planning takes place and a good understanding of the times and seasons. For instance, mums with young children need to spend the early years with their children. Honestly, time does fly, and before you know it, the youngsters running around the house will soon become adults on their way to boarding school, college, university or to their own home. It is therefore pertinent to make good use of the time we have with them.

Chapter Nine

Spending time with our children is a rewarding experience which has no price tag. Time spent can be as simple as watching their favourite TV programme with them or reading a book together.

You may say spending time with our children sounds good, but how do we get rid of the weights or the 'too many or too much syndrome'?

Well, before saying yes to the next social event or assignment, ask yourself the following:-

* Is it important?

* Would it add to me or take from me?

* Will my absence be noticed?

* Have I been out every weekend this month?

* Can I attend with my children?

* Have I spent quality time with my children this week or month?

* Have I rested this month?

Also before you speak endlessly on the phone, ask yourself the following:-

- Have I done all my motherly duties?

- Is this conversation building me up or just mere chatter?

- Is there something else I should be doing?

- Have I given my children my undivided attention today?

- Could I be resting now?

Learning to stop or halt would also halt stress but taking on more than can be managed would lead to more stress.

What Some Mums Did

Juliet tried so hard to get rid of excesses at a point in her life. As a single mum, she always felt the need to socialise to seemingly get her life back on track and maybe meet someone new. Though her intentions were right, it became a 'too much or too many syndrome' with Juliet attending a social event every weekend. With this lifestyle, she had to deal with grumpy and tired children continuously; face a disorganised day and then struggle to drag her tired body around the following week. Other significant issues began to stem from her lifestyle such as impatience, nagging, shouting, no strength, and no time to bond with her children. However, Juliet began to cut down on her social activities to have time for herself and her children.

Lade had her issues too. She struggled with this technological age. Though a stay-at-home mum, she spent an incredible number of hours sat watching TV or chatting endlessly online. She had failed to do what was important or needful and struggled to cramp her daily chores into the hours she had left. This time wastage left Lade stressed and on edge, being incapable of coping with any form of pressure, especially the continuous banter from her three-year-old. Once she dealt with her excesses, she used her time wisely. She began to set time aside to work, rest and bond with her family.

Chapter Nine

With Nola, the story was different. She had formed the habit of bringing work home or staying extra hours at work, which gave her live-in-nanny sole responsibility of her children. Thankfully, she decided to turn a new leaf once she realised her body and mind was crying out for help. She began to treat her home as a place to wind down and relax, while the office was the place to do all the work. This change made a huge difference in her home, and she began to give her children her undivided attention whenever she was home.

Action Plan

❀ Plan your time wisely.

❀ Cut down on unnecessary phone calls.

❀ Cut down on excessive social engagements.

❀ Cut down on the hours spent in front of the TV.

❀ Try multitasking; for example, you can wash the dishes while having a casual conversation with a friend using the speaker of the phone or earphones. You can also try watching your favourite programme while ironing clothes. Multitasking helps us to perform tasks while doing what we love, in order words, killing two birds with a stone.

❀ Learn to say No, especially when you have no time or energy.

❀ Remember to spend some time every day on yourself and your family.

❀ Write down three things that prevent you from spending time with your children and yourself, and work at eliminating them.

Chapter Nine

Personal Notes

Chapter Ten

*Pray
without ceasing
**1 Thessalonians 5:17
(KJV)***

Pray

I have saved the best for last. Having laid down practical steps on how to manage stress, this chapter focuses on the all-important, which is PRAYER.

As a young Christian woman, I have learnt that there is nothing I can do without prayer. I had known since giving my life to Jesus Christ that "a prayerless Christian is a powerless Christian"; however, this realisation further hit home when I started my own family. At first, I thought I would have to use my strength to manage my children and my home. This ideology was certainly the highway to stress, chaos and disaster; but fortunately for me, I quickly changed my course, thanks to sound advice from my mum.

It was about the time when I was to have my first child, and of course, mum came round to help me. I learnt a lot about motherhood from her. She prayed about every "little" thing. It was a case of "if it was not going according to plan, then it was worth talking to God about". Even after I had my child, we still prayed about all sorts. Every detail of each day was committed to God in prayer – cooking times, meal times, bath time, nap time, crying times; God had to take absolute control.

However, when I fell pregnant with my second child things took a different turn. I was consumed with worry. How was I going to cope with two children under the age of two? As an organised person, I certainly wasn't prepared for this additional gift. Unfortunately, the doctor's report did not help matters. There was always something negative to say. I began to focus more on the issues rather than on praying to God. It was a challenging season in my life, and I, unfortunately, allowed it.

Receive this truth: Whatever you forbid on earth will be considered to be forbidden in heaven and whatever you release on earth will be considered to be released in heaven.
- Matthew 18:18 (TPT)

In that season, I was not 'forbidding or releasing' anything, and unfortunately, I was too scared to tell anyone what I was going through. I guess I was overwhelmed, and during all the turmoil, I forgot the efficacy of prayer.

I think I became numb, and I cried most times. I certainly bottled all my worries to myself. No one, not even my husband knew the struggles on my inside.

May we never forget that the Lord works wonders for every one of his devoted lovers. And this is how I know that he will answer my every prayer. -Psalm 4:3 (TPT)

Dear mum, I pray that we will never forget that God answers

prayers. Even during storms, please never forget to call on God. Even when there is a human to turn to, first turn to God.

I must confess that there was a noticeable difference when I compared my times of prayer to the times of prayerlessness. I somehow went back to talking to God. I don't know when but I eventually did, and He truly stepped in to put order back in my life.

Call upon Me in the day of trouble; I will deliver you, and you shall glorify Me."Psalm 50:15 (NKJV)

I now had a better understanding of why I had to pray about every "little" thing. Some things did not change, but I was able to handle the trials that came my way better. There were days when all I could do was to cry before God. On some days, I would dance before His presence while on others; I would sit quietly listening to gospel music. I had no prescriptive way to commune with God, but I made sure I did.

Through God's help, I coped well with the early stages of motherhood. Planning and setting routines began to come naturally to me, yet I was going through a trying period.

My second child was poorly at birth, so we had to pay weekly visits to two different hospitals, in two different cities. But, this was my testimony. I still cannot comprehend how I managed to care for my first child who was a year and nine months old, comfort a poorly baby, manage my home, care for my husband and self. I must confess that talking to God like a friend next to me, helped me.

In that season, I learnt that telling God just how I felt, helped me. Some days were 'numb days', and all I could mutter were the words, 'Lord help me'.

Prayer made me better equipped to cope with what life suddenly threw at me as a mother of two babies. I understood that it was my responsibility from God to give them a good start in life, and I could only do this through God's help.

Prayer gave me hope when I thought there was no way out. It turned my life around, made me smile again and stay sane amid real trouble. That is the power of prayer.

I had many reasons to thank God despite the doctor's negative report. Some of these reports did not become a reality – thanks to God. On the other hand, some reports were not as bad as medical science had stated. Again I say, I had many reasons to thank God in the storm.

My fellow believers, when it seems as though you are facing nothing but difficulties see it as an invaluable opportunity to experience the greatest joy that you can! For you know that

when your faith is tested it stirs up power within you to endure all things. - James 1:2-3 (TPT)

Prayer need not be complicated but should be as truthful and straightforward as possible. I choose to define prayer as talking and listening to God. I see it as a way of developing a meaningful relationship with our Maker by having a consistent, honest conversation with Him. I see prayer as a well where I draw strength and direction from God.

Over the years, I have had a large number of mums complain about the same thing;

"My prayer life is non-existent."

I have also had others ask this simple question;

"How can I pray when I have young children?"

It is quite challenging for mums to develop a vibrant prayer life while caring for young children. I had that challenge too. It became extremely difficult to have a dedicated period for my quiet time, and it was much more challenging to pray for long hours until I got the revelation to 'pray-on-the-go'.

Praying-on-the-go is a simple and conscious practice to pray while completing tasks or as you go about daily routines (my

definition). I realised that I could never find time for this spiritual exercise, so I associated prayer with set tasks.
How did I do this?

I prayed for the children when I bathed them or when I fed them. I prayed for myself and my spiritual life when I had a bath. I prayed for my home when I cleaned the house. I prayed for my husband when I made the family meals. I prayed for others when I did the laundry, and I worshipped and sang to God when I did the dishes.

It started as practice sessions, but as they say 'practice makes perfect'. I carried on with this but had to make adjustments as the children got older. I no longer bath them, but I pray for them when I do their laundry or help comb their hair.

Praying-on-the-go was embedded on my midnight trips to the toilet. I always made a detour to the children's room to say a word of prayer over them.

Apart from praying for our wants, children and families, our prayers must also include thanksgiving. Just like the story of the ten lepers in the Bible, the only one that returned to say thank you to Jesus became whole.

And one of them, when he saw that he was healed, turned back, and with a loud voice glorified God, And fell down on

---

his face at his feet, giving him thanks: and he was a Samaritan. And Jesus answering said, Were there not ten cleansed? but where are the nine? There are not found that returned to give glory to God, save this stranger. And he said unto him, Arise, go thy way: thy faith hath made thee whole.
- Luke 17:15-19 (KJV)

Our gratitude and thanksgiving to God will create an atmosphere for Him to complete the good work He has started in our lives as mothers.

We must thank God for the status of motherhood and for the opportunity to be called mother. If we have not looked around lately, it is about time we stop and notice the many women around us that desire to be mothers and are still waiting on God for the fruit of the womb. We should pause to thank God for motherhood, which is a privilege and not a right.

We should also thank God for the gift of life to nurture and raise the children we have.

So how can prayer alleviate stress?

Pour out all your worries and stress upon him and leave them there, for he always tenderly cares for you. - 1 Peter 5:7 (TPT)

And if anyone longs to be wise, ask God for wisdom and he will give it! He won't see your lack of wisdom as an

opportunity to scold you over your failures but he will overwhelm your failures with his generous grace.
- James 1:5 (TPT)

I must say that wisdom is the principal thing (Proverbs 4:7). We need knowledge, wisdom and understanding to manage the early stages of motherhood and cope with stress effectively. As mothers, we should prayerfully ask God for wisdom on how to get rid of stress.

Once we have the overwhelming feeling of stress, it is crucial to ask God for strength to cope with the situation. Praying about situations does guarantee a change which may not be instant. But keep on believing. Be hopeful that a change will occur. That is the prayer of faith.

We must be consistent in prayer. It would be most effective if prayer is said before problems arise. We can achieve this when prayer becomes a lifestyle.

The heartfelt and persistent prayer of a righteous man (believer) can accomplish much [when put into action and made effective by God—it is dynamic and can have tremendous power]. - James 5:16b (Amplified Bible)

Concerning this book, here are a few points to pray about:-
Dear God, teach me to plan my time better and help me to

prioritise accordingly. *Ecclesiastes 3:1 (New King James Version)*

🌸 Dear God, help me to bring up my children according to your will, through the boundaries I set. *Proverbs 10:1* and *Proverbs 29:15 & 17 (New Living Translation).*

🌸 Dear God, let the fruit of my lips be pleasing and full of life always. *Proverbs 15:4 and Proverbs 31:26 (New Living Translation).*

🌸 Dear God, direct my steps to the right childcare provider. *Psalm 37:23 (New Living Translation)*

🌸 Dear God, show me the things that bring stress into my life. *Daniel 2:28a (New Living Translation)*

🌸 Dear God, I pray that all those who come in contact with my children will be positive influences .e.g. teachers, carers, friends, and even yourself. *Proverbs 13:20 and 1 Corinthians 15:33 (New International Version)*

🌸 Dear God, please help me to be a good role model for my children. *Psalm 101:2 (The Passion Translation)*

🌸 Dear God, please make me a joyful mother of children. *Psalm 113:9 (The Passion Translation)*

There are a host of other things we should pray about; however, if prayer is treated as everyday conversation, then most of our issues would be addressed.

I read this beautiful poem which encapsulates the essence of being a praying mother.

I HAVE A MOTHER THAT PRAYS
(Author Unknown)

Some have had kings in their lineage,
Some to whom honour was paid.
I don't have those as my ancestors
But I have a mother who prays.

I have a mother who prays for me
And pleads with the Lord every day for me.
Oh what a difference it makes for me
I have a mother who prays.
My mother's prayers cannot save me,
Only mine can avail;
But Mother introduced me to someone,
someone who never could fail.

Oh yes, I have a mother who prays for me
And pleads with the Lord every day for me.
O what a difference it makes for me
I have a mother who prays.

Action Plan

* Read Christian books on prayer to help ignite your prayer life.

* Look and learn from praying mothers around you.

* Check out what the Bible says about joy and peace.

* Set some time apart from now to pray for your children and your role as a mother. It can be at a specific time each day or a particular day in the week.

* Remember to combine your prayers with faith and action

* Pray! Pray! Pray

After all, is being said and done, I pray that this book has been a blessing to you. No one knows how best to lay the foundation for our children, apart from God. He teaches and expects those that have learnt to help others.

I pray that each day comes with the grace to eliminate stress in our lives. Keep shining, keep rising and continue to be the best STRESS FREE MUM that God intended.

Personal Notes